WHAT IS FEAR?

An Introduction to Feelings

What is FEAR?

An Introduction to Feelings

By Jean Rosenbaum, M.D. and Lutie McAuliffe

Illustrations by Tomie de Paola

PRENTICE-HALL, INC.
Englewood Cliffs, N.J.

What Is Fear? An Introduction to Feelings
by Jean Rosenbaum and Lutie McAuliffe

Printed in the United States of America
10   9   8   7   6   5   4   3   2
Prentice-Hall International, Inc., London
Prentice-Hall of Australia, Pty. Ltd., North Sydney
Prentice-Hall of Canada, Ltd., Toronto
Prentice-Hall of India Private Ltd. New Delhi
Prentice-Hall of Japan, Inc., Tokyo

Library of Congress Cataloging in Publication Data
Rosenbaum, Jean.
    What is fear.
SUMMARY: Explores the nature of fear and anxiety
through case histories and discusses ways of dealing
with these emotions.
    1. Anxiety—Juvenile literature. [1. Fear.
2. Emotions] I. McAuliffe, Lutie, date   joint
author. II. De Paola, Thomas Anthony, illus.
                III.   Title.
RC531.R66   616.8'522   72–3226
            ISBN 0–13–952283–2

To Sigrid, for her patience and help

Introduction

This is a book about fear. It describes how fear can help you and how it can hurt you. It introduces ways of understanding and handling fear. Everyone in the world has felt fear. But you'd be surprised how many people are ashamed of their fears. They think they're weird, crazy, terrible.

We don't want you to think your fears are strange and horrible, because they're not. No matter what fear you have, no matter how childish, terrible, silly or crazy you think it is—thousands of people, young and old, have the same kinds of fears as you. The person who brags, "I've never been afraid" is really just ashamed of his fears. He thinks he's got to hide them because they're so silly or terrible.

But if you hide fear it can hurt you. Fear doesn't go away just because you pretend it isn't there. It can make you feel sick. It can cause you to get bad grades or lose friends. But most of all it can make you lonely and unhappy.

In other words, hidden fears are your enemy. They're your enemy because they prevent you from doing things you *have* to do and things you *want* to do.

The only way to overcome fear is to know about it. What it is. Where it comes from. How it works. Then you can handle it.

This book presents the most common fears of children—the ones you're likely to have. And it explains the most common reasons for these fears. It will help you think about and get to know the things that scare you. It is a book for sharing with parents, relatives, teachers or friends.

We would like you to share it. There are many ideas in this book which will probably be new and strange to you. Talking about new ideas, particularly with adults, can be very helpful in getting them straight.

Because fear and its causes can be hard to understand, some of the ideas are repeated a number of times throughout the book, but in different ways, so they will become familiar, comfortable and easy to work with.

This book does not have to be read straight through. You can skip to the Chapters which interest you most and then go back and read the rest. We do recommend that you read the whole book, however, because understanding fear helps in understanding other people.

CONTENTS

CHAPTER ONE

WHAT IS FEAR?

Fear is the feeling you get when you think you're in danger. It's the emotion that tells you, "Hey! Something bad is about to happen. I'd better protect myself."

"If I don't study for that test, I'm going to fail."

"I'd better go home now. I'm afraid to ride my bike in the dark without headlights."

"I don't care what Jerry says! I'm not going to play in that abandoned building. I could really get hurt if an old board came loose and fell on me."

1

"When Mom finds out I've lied to her, she's going to be furious. Maybe I'd better tell her the truth."

Sometimes it's hard to understand that fear is a very helpful, necessary emotion. Fear can make you sweat, giggle, tremble, stutter, cry and even wet your pants. Naturally, these things can be embarrassing.

But the important thing to remember is that fear is your warning system. It alerts you to dangerous situations. Without it, you wouldn't know when to protect yourself. So people who say they have never been afraid are lying. Everyone feels fear. These people are just too embarrassed to admit it.

What should you do when you're afraid?

First, you should figure out what kind of danger you're facing. What are you really afraid of? What can this thing or person or situation actually do to you? Is it *likely* to do anything? *Are you really in danger?*

Once you know what you're up against, you can feel confident. You know what's likely to happen and you can then do something about it.

This is the simplest way to handle fear. Greg's story is a good example.

Greg was nine years old. On his way to school there was a house, which was guarded by a large, fierce dog. Whenever Greg went by the house, the dog growled, showed his teeth and followed Greg down the block. Greg was terrified of this dog.

One day Greg and his mother were walking by the house where the dog lived. The dog ran toward them and Greg froze. He wanted to pretend he wasn't afraid but he was so scared he couldn't move.

"What's the matter?" asked his mother.

"That dog's going to bite me!" cried Greg.

"No, he won't," said his mother. "Don't be afraid."

"Yes, he will! He growls at me and shows his teeth everytime he sees me."

"That's because you're a stranger," said Greg's mother. "This dog has been trained to scare away strangers. But once he gets to know you, he won't bother you anymore. You'll see."

The next day Greg's mother took Greg to visit the Nicholsons, the family who owned the dog. Greg fed the dog and played with him.

After that, the dog barked occasionally at Greg but Greg wasn't afraid. He knew the dog wouldn't bite him.

So Greg's fear helped him. It warned him that he might be in danger. If Greg had found out that the dog actually was dangerous, then he could have taken steps to protect himself. He could have asked his parents for help.

Sometimes, though, we are afraid *even when we know we're not in danger*. Everyone has had this experience. There are days when we just feel afraid. We may worry about harmless things like bugs, or non-existent things like ghosts, or unlikely events like fires. Or we may just feel nervous and tense, as though something bad is about to happen.

Are these fears different from Greg's?

They certainly are. Greg was afraid because he had reasons to think the dog might hurt him. The dog growled and showed his teeth.

But worrying about harmless, unlikely or non-existent things is a different problem. Then we aren't in danger. We just *feel* as though we are.

This feeling of fear, even though we aren't in danger,

is called anxiety. Anxiety is much more common than you might think. After all, we aren't in *real* danger very often. Yet many times we feel afraid for no obvious reasons.

How does anxiety get started?

When a person feels anxious, he is afraid of his own feelings. He may be angry, for instance, and think it's wrong to feel anger. He may try to hide his anger. But his anger won't go away just because he pretends it isn't there. It will stay inside and make him afraid—afraid that one day his anger will explode and cause him to hurt someone.

Usually there is no reason to be so frightened of your own feelings. Even though they may seem very powerful and awful, there are ways of expressing them without hurting anyone.

The trick is to find out what you really feel. This can be hard. Your feelings may frighten you so much you're afraid to think about them. In this case it's best to talk to someone you trust. Your parents. A relative. Someone at school. Anyone who can help you feel confident enough to think about what's bothering you. The story of Caroline shows how talking about feelings can help overcome anxiety.

Caroline was eight years old. She worried all the time about getting dirty. She believed that dirt was full of germs and disease. The only way to keep from getting sick, Caroline thought, was to be spotlessly clean.

Of course, Caroline couldn't keep that clean. She would have had to spend all day washing and changing her clothes. So she worried. And when she accidently did get dirty, she felt small and scared as though something terrible was about to happen.

4

Naturally Caroline never felt happy. She had no idea why she was so full of fear. She knew it didn't make any sense to be so worried about germs, but she couldn't stop.

Caroline's teacher, Miss Larson, noticed how unhappy Caroline looked and she decided to talk to Caroline's mother. Caroline's mother said, "I've noticed it too. But when I try to find out what's wrong, Caroline just says, 'Nothing.' "

"Sometimes it's hard to talk about fears," said Miss Larson. She understood that fears are often caused by feelings we're afraid to express. "But if you like, maybe I can try to find out what's making Caroline so unhappy."

For the next few months, Miss Larson spent a lot of time making friends with Caroline. Gradually Caroline began to trust her. And one day after school, she stayed to talk to Miss Larson. Miss Larson asked her why she seemed so nervous all the time.

"I don't know," said Caroline, feeling very embarrassed. But after she talked for a few more minutes she thought of a reason. "I always wonder if I'm going to get sick," she said. "I just seem to get dirty and germy whatever I do."

"Well, you know," said Miss Larson, "keeping clean is a good idea. But you can't be spotless all the time."

"But you have to be clean!" argued Caroline. "Think of all the germs that are around. If you don't wash them off they'll make you sick."

"Do you get sick often?" Miss Larson asked

"No," said Caroline.

"Then I don't think a little dirt is going to hurt you."

"But getting dirty is so awful!" Caroline cried.

"How do you feel when you get dirty?" Miss Larson asked.

Caroline wasn't sure she wanted to talk about this. But she'd been so miserable for so long that she decided she wanted to tell someone.

"I feel—well, I think I'm going to get sick or something. I feel like something awful is going to happen to me. Maybe that sounds silly."

"It's not silly," said Miss Larson. "When a person is afraid there's always a reason. And if you really think hard about it, maybe you can find out why dirt scares you."

For the next two weeks Caroline thought about the problem. Then, one night, she spilled some dirt from a flowerpot onto her dress.

"Caroline!" her mother cried. "You're *always* doing that. Change your dress right away!"

The next day Caroline told Miss Larson what had happened. "My mother was really mad at me," she said. "She always gets mad when I do something wrong."

"Do you think getting dirty is wrong?" asked Miss Larson.

"I don't know," said Caroline. "I guess so."

"And how do you feel when your mother yells at you?"

"Pretty awful," said Caroline. "I feel like . . ." and then Caroline started to cry.

You see, Caroline's parents scolded her a lot. Sometimes when she deserved it. But many times they yelled at her for things she couldn't help, like getting dirty occasionally.

Caroline dreaded these scoldings. She tried to please

her parents. But no matter what she did, it never seemed good enough and this made Caroline very angry.

"Why do my parents always pick on me!" she thought. "I can't do anything right. They're always yelling at me. I hate them."

Part of Caroline wanted very much to hurt her parents. But part of her loved them and didn't want to hurt them at all. So her angry feelings made her very afraid. What if her angry feelings accidently got out and she hurt her parents—without really meaning to? Caroline didn't want to think about this. So she buried her anger way in the back of her mind. But she couldn't bury it completely. She remembered it everytime she saw something her parents hated, like dirt.

This is why Caroline was afraid of dirt. Dirt reminded her of the thing she really feared—her own feelings.

Once Caroline realized that anger didn't make her into a monster, she didn't feel so anxious about dirt—or anything else her parents didn't like. And when her parents made her angry, she would explain to them how she felt. Sometimes they would agree that they had been unfair because they were tired or worried about their own problems. But sometimes they wouldn't.

In this case, Caroline would still be angry but she didn't feel frightened by that anger anymore. She learned to take her feelings out on things she couldn't hurt. She kicked her toys. She threw rocks in vacant lots. She went into her room and pounded on her pillow. She drew funny pictures of her parents, which expressed how she felt.

So Caroline solved her problem. She learned about

her feelings, just like Greg learned about the snarling dog. She found out they weren't dangerous and that she could express them without hurting anybody.

With a little help, everyone can learn about his fears. Everyone can learn to handle powerful emotions, rather than pretending they aren't there. Then we can enjoy ourselves and not be afraid of feelings, people and situations which aren't really dangerous.

CHAPTER TWO

FEAR OF THE DARK

Many children are afraid of the dark. But many adults are afraid of the dark, too. It's very natural to fear darkness.

Think about how you feel in the dark. You feel alone —you can't see anyone. You feel clumsy—you're likely to trip over something and fall. You can't find things and it's hard to move around. You feel helpless—and you *are* more physically helpless than you would be if the lights were on.

Probably, though, you *feel* more alone and helpless

than you really are. This is because you remember your first experience with darkness as a baby.

When you were a baby, darkness seemed really dangerous. You were too small to take care of yourself. You depended on your parents for everything. In the dark, your parents were gone. If you needed them, you couldn't get out of bed and find them. All you could do was cry and hope they'd come.

Just because you're older now, doesn't mean you automatically feel less helpless than you did as a baby. Many people feel alone and helpless, no matter how old they are. This is why many people, old and young, are afraid of the dark.

Darkness makes people more physically helpless than they would be if the lights were on. This physical helplessness *reminds* them of all the lonely, helpless feelings they have inside but are afraid to talk about or even think about. The story of Grace is a good example of how this works.

When Grace was little, both her parents worked and she was left with many different baby-sitters. Grace didn't like her sitters very much. She wanted to be with her parents, not with them. But her parents weren't there so Grace felt very lonely. She began to worry that no one cared about her.

Grace also felt very helpless. She wanted her parents to stay home but they couldn't. They had to work because they needed the money. Grace really didn't understand this. She was too little. All she knew was that her parents weren't there and there was nothing she could do about it.

At night, Grace would not sleep with the lights off.

She'd say, "Don't turn the lights off! There's a big bear under my bed and he'll come out and eat me up if you turn off the lights."

Her parents tried to convince her that there wasn't any bear under her bed. But Grace wouldn't listen. Darkness made her feel so lonely and scared she was sure there actually had to be something dangerous in her room.

It's easy to see why Grace felt this way. In the dark, her parents were gone. She couldn't even see her toys. She couldn't move around very well. She felt totally alone and helpless. This *reminded* her of her growing fear that nobody really cared about her—that someday her parents would go off to work and never come back.

As Grace got older, things didn't get much better. She had playmates at school, but after school she was often alone. Her parents didn't get home until 6 o'clock and then they were tired from working. They didn't have the energy to play with Grace. And Grace grew more afraid of the dark.

She began to have nightmares. In her dreams she could see the ground opening up and horrible goblins crawling out. She would try to run but she couldn't get away. The goblins were reaching for her and her legs wouldn't move.

Grace never told her parents about these dreams. She never told them how miserable, lonely and afraid she was. In fact, she hardly ever thought about it. She couldn't. She was just too angry.

Deep down inside, Grace was actually furious with her parents for leaving her every day. But she couldn't admit it. What would they think if they found out that she wanted to scream and throw things at them? Grace believed they would abandon her. She thought she *deserved* to be abandoned because she was so angry.

This is why Grace had nightmares. A nightmare is a bad dream. Like all dreams, it's caused by the thoughts and feelings we have in our minds when we go to sleep.

When Grace went to sleep her mind was filled with the fear that she would be left alone and helpless. So she dreamed that there was no one to help her and no way to escape—even when goblins attacked.

Grace's nightmares didn't come from watching horror movies or reading ghost stories. They came from the fears she was afraid to think about. The goblins were really no different from the bear she had imagined when she was younger. Both expressed her fear that she was in great danger of being left alone and helpless.

But let's imagine that Grace had not grown up afraid and angry. Let's say she felt protected and loved. Then she might have seen the night as a very peaceful time. "I can't see in the dark," she might have said to herself, "but neither can anyone else. So we all share the same problem. Besides it's so quiet and peaceful at night, I really like it."

Eventually, Grace did begin to feel more comfortable in the dark. As she got older she began to help with the housework. Sometimes she cooked dinner and had it waiting for her parents when they got home. This made her feel more like part of the family. It also made things easier for her parents and they, in turn, had more time and energy for Grace.

Then when Grace got to Junior High, she made several close friends. She trusted them. They cared about her. And Grace realized she didn't have to wait for her parents to give her attention and love. She could go out and find it. She could make friends. She wasn't nearly as helpless as she thought!

Most important, Grace began to talk about her feelings. First to her friends and later to her parents. She discovered that neither her parents nor her friends would abandon her because of what she felt. If she became angry with them, they might get angry back—but they wouldn't stop loving her.

So Grace got over her fear of the dark. She found out that she was not alone. She was not helpless. Anger did not make her into a monster.

Grace also learned that parents are human too. They have problems and worries. Sometimes they're not able to give all the attention we want. But that doesn't mean they don't love us or that they'll abandon us.

Grace learned all of this because she opened up to other people. They opened up to her in return. Then she saw she didn't have to be frightened of her feelings —or of other people's. There was no reason for her to be afraid of the dark.

CHAPTER THREE

FEAR OF STRANGERS

Fear of strangers is a lot like fear of the dark. Neither strangers nor darkness are dangerous. Yet both can make you *feel* as though you're in danger. Why? Think about it this way.

When you were a baby you couldn't get along without your parents. You didn't want anyone to come between you and them. When strangers were around, you probably thought, "Who are these large people? What are they doing in my house? Are they going to hurt me and my parents? Are they going to take my parents away from me?"

And in a way, strangers did take your parents away from you. They took some of your parents' attention when you wanted it all for yourself. As a baby, this made you feel helpless and afraid—afraid that someday a stranger would take your parents away forever and there wouldn't be anything you could do about it.

Then as you got older, you could do more things for yourself. You didn't feel so helpless. So you stopped being upset that your parents spent time with strangers. You had your friends. They had their friends. And you still had each other.

There are some children, though, who don't grow out of their fear of strangers. Even though they know strangers aren't dangerous, they're still afraid. This is anxiety at work. Let's see what happened in Terry's case.

Terry was ten years old and he was very afraid of strangers. He was afraid to make friends with the kids at school. He shied away from his teachers. He couldn't make himself try out for the fifth grade soccer team. He pretended he was sick so he wouldn't have to go on the class trip.

At home Terry spent most of his time reading and watching television. He also used to daydream a lot. Sometimes he would pretend that he was a rock star and that thousands of people adored him. Other times he would imagine that he was very sick and the whole world was praying for him to recover. But the truth was that Terry didn't even have one friend to sit next to on the school bus.

What was Terry's problem?

Actually Terry was a lot like Grace. Both of them felt alone and helpless. Grace, because her parents had to work. Terry, because his parents had a lot of friends and loved to give parties. With the house full of strangers, Terry felt left out. He thought his parents would never like him as much as they liked their friends.

Because his parents seemed to ignore him, Terry was afraid that everyone else would too. "After all," Terry figured, "my parents are *supposed* to love me. That's their job."

Terry didn't know he felt this way. He avoided thinking about it. But just the same he kept away from strangers. He didn't want them to leave him and go off with someone else, just the way his parents seemed to.

One day Terry's parents were giving a large party. As the first guests arrived, Terry began to feel very frightened. Though he knew he had no reason to be afraid, he ran out the back door and around to the side of the house.

Up under the eaves there was a wasp's nest. Terry's father had warned him about it. Now Terry forgot it was there and ran underneath it, barefoot. He stepped on a wasp and it stung him.

The sting hurt so much Terry limped back to the kitchen where his mother was getting cups for her guests. "Terry, what's wrong?" she asked. Terry told her. "You poor kid," she said and she gave him a kiss and began to fix his foot.

Just then, some of the guests came into the kitchen. Terry's mother introduced them. Terry managed a smile and a few words. He was surprised to discover that the guests were friendly to him.

For the rest of the party, Terry felt like staying around his parents. He helped them by collecting the used cups and ashtrays. He even talked to some of the guests.

When the last guest left, Terry's father took the family to a drive-in restaurant. Terry felt as though he was being rewarded. "Are you glad I came to your party?" he asked.

"Of course," said Terry's father. "You were a big help."

"And the guests all thought you were wonderful," said Terry's mother.

This made Terry feel better, for the moment. It didn't cure his fear of strangers but it did make him feel a little less lonely and helpless.

One thing, though, still puzzled Terry. Why had he felt so frightened when the first guests arrived? Why had he run under the wasp's nest when he *knew* it was there?

The truth was that Terry had hoped he'd be stung! Then his parents would have to take care of him and ignore their guests.

When his parents *did* pay attention to him, Terry felt better. Why? Because the guests only *reminded* him of the thing he really feared—the lonely, helpless feeling he had inside. When his parents showed their love for him, Terry's loneliness went away for a while and so did his fear of strangers.

If Terry could have told his parents what was wrong, he might have spared himself a lot of pain. If he could have said, "Please don't forget about me. I need you. I want us to be together and be a real family," his parents might have given up some of their parties and spent more time with him.

But Terry didn't. And every time his parents didn't show their love for him, he felt afraid of strangers.

It wasn't until Terry got older that he began to see how much fun and friends he was missing because he was afraid of strangers. So he talked to his school counselors and teachers about his problems. Through these talks he learned a lot.

He realized that he was afraid of strangers because he thought they would ignore him as his parents sometimes did. He also learned that he wasn't as alone and helpless as he thought he was. There were many people who were willing to listen to him and love him. All he had to do was ask strangers to be his friend. Strangers could give him the attention he didn't get from his parents.

So fear of strangers is caused by hidden feelings. Sometimes it's a feeling of being alone and helpless. Sometimes it's anger that is the real problem.

Let's say you're a very normal kind of person and you get angry a lot—at many different people. You get angry at your mother for making you study. At your father for making you cut the grass. At your teacher for punishing you. At your friends for teasing you. At your sister because she's younger and gets away with murder.

Let's say you think it's wrong to get angry. You feel other people won't like you if they find out how you feel. So you try to hide it.

But trying to hide anger just makes you angrier—because it makes you feel helpless. Not only are all those people bothering you but you're such a helpless nobody you can't do anything to stop them! Or so you think.

Now you are more angry than you were before. But

you still won't admit how you feel. So what do you do? You're likely to say, "Who me? I'm not angry. It's all those other people. They're the ones who are angry at me. That's why they always pick on me. They hate me."

This is called projection. It's a very common thing people do when they are afraid to admit how they feel. It's like being a movie projector.

The film (your feelings) is inside you but you beam it onto a screen (other people). You forget you are the one who is angry. And you begin to think that the people with whom you are angry, are actually angry with you.

Projection is also like putting on colored glasses. If you feel blue, the world seems sad and blue. If you're angry and you're "seeing red,"the world looks fiery and angry. This is exactly what happened to Roger and it caused his fear of strangers.

When Roger was little, his parents used to fight a lot. They argued about a great many things, but particularly about their relatives.

Their relatives lived nearby and often came to visit. This would have been fine, except that the relatives criticized nearly everything Roger's parents tried to do. And after they left, Roger's parents would get into a big fight over what had been said.

"Your mother should shut up!" Roger's father would shout. "She's always sticking her nose into our business!"

"My mother isn't as bad as your father!" Roger's mother would say. "If your father makes one more crack about my cooking I'm going to sock him!"

And so it would go. Between the fighting and the visiting, Roger didn't get very much attention. This made him furious. But he was afraid to tell his parents how angry he was with them. He felt that if he complained, his parents would spend even *less* time with him. So Roger kept quiet. And instead of feeling angry with his parents, he took his anger out on his relatives. It was all their fault!

Now when the relatives came over, Roger wouldn't say hello. He wouldn't even smile. He always seemed to be spilling things on them or stepping on their toes. (Roger didn't realize that this was his way of getting back at them for taking up so much of his parents' time and causing so many fights.)

Then one day when Roger was about four years old, his uncle gave him the car keys to play with and Roger lost them. He didn't lose the keys on purpose. His anger had simply made him "forget" where he put them—just as you might forget to do something you're angry about having to do, like taking out the garbage.

When Roger's uncle discovered that the keys were lost he became very angry—for the moment. He had an important appointment and he needed his car. He was fuming. "If I were your father," he said to Roger, "I'd teach you a lesson you'd never forget!"

This frightened Roger. He thought that now all his relatives *knew* how angry he was with them. He was sure that in return they would be very angry with him and punish him if he ever showed his anger toward them again. This meant Roger could no longer get back at his relatives by spilling things on them and stepping on their toes. He had to pretend he liked them! At least that's what he thought.

Now Roger was in a very difficult spot. He couldn't admit he was angry with his parents and he couldn't show he was angry with his relatives. What could he do with all the anger he was feeling?

He projected it. Roger decided that he wasn't angry at all. It was the rest of the world! They were the ones who were angry and at any moment, they might become angry with him.

Naturally this idea frightened Roger and made him genuinely afraid of strangers. He was terrified of people in stores. On buses he clung to his mother to avoid even brushing up against a stranger. He hated school and kicked up such a fuss that his teacher advised his parents to take him to a psychiatrist. A psychiatrist is a doctor who helps people who are unhappy because of feelings they're afraid to admit, even to themselves.

Roger's psychiatrist talked to Roger the way Miss Larson talked to Caroline. He tried to get Roger to think about his feelings. Slowly Roger began to see how angry he was. Then, instead of projecting his anger onto strangers who had nothing to do with it, he told his parents how he felt about their fighting and about the relatives.

After that Roger felt much closer to his parents. They understood how he felt and they worked to change the things which were bothering him. This meant that Roger no longer had to hide his feelings.

Another hidden feeling that causes fear of strangers is shame. Shame is the feeling we get when we think we've done something wrong. Often when people are ashamed, they try to hide what they've done so that other people won't think bad things about them or punish them.

For example: If Bobby breaks his mother's best vase, he might try to throw away the pieces so his mother won't find out. Or he might tell his mother the cat knocked it over.

But even if Bobby lies about what happened to the vase, he's still going to feel guilty about having broken it. On top of that, he is probably going to be afraid that someone will find out he has lied.

So shame can put us in a bad position. It can make us hide our problems and therefore prevent people from finding out what is the matter and helping us. It can also make us feel bad about ourselves for no good reason at all. This is particularly true for children who are curious about sex.

As a child is growing up, he wants to examine his body and the bodies of other people. A boy wants to know how he is different from a girl and a girl is curious about how she's different from a boy. Both boys and girls want to know what grownup bodies look like.

Some children satisfy this curiosity by peeking at others while they are dressing. Others play games where each child has a chance to look at or touch another child. Others spend time touching their own bodies. And others just think a lot about what it will be like to be sexually mature and to have a family.

But many children are ashamed of these thoughts and actions. They think it is wrong to be sexually curious. They are afraid to ask their parents or teachers how babies are born and why girls are different from boys. They don't understand that sexual curiosity is part of growing up and that no one should be ashamed of wanting to know about his or her body. Let's take the case of Sandy to explore how sexual curiosity can lead to shame, and shame can lead to fear of strangers.

When Sandy was eleven, her mother got very sick. She had to stay in the hospital for a month. Sandy was "grown up for her age" so she and her father took care of the house, while her mother was away.

Taking care of the house was quite a job, since Sandy had four younger brothers and sisters. But she had helped her mother before and knew how to do it. And even though she had to work hard, there were some good things about filling in for her mother.

Her brothers and sisters looked up to her. Now that her mother was gone, she was the center of their attention. And they had to do whatever she told them to.

Her father paid a lot of attention to her, too. Sometimes he even asked her advice. Sandy felt like a very important person.

Sandy decided that having a family was a lot of fun. She could hardly wait to get married and have children of her own. "I wish I would grow up," she thought over and over. "I wish I weren't just a little girl."

Sometimes, alone in her room, Sandy would take off her clothes and look at her body. She tried to imagine what it would look like when she was fully grown. Sometimes she would close her eyes and wish as hard as she could that her body would change, but, of course, it stayed the same.

Sandy thought and thought about being a mother. She found a book about the way children are born and read it over and over. And because she wanted children so much, Sandy almost convinced herself that her brothers and sisters were really *her* children. She felt as if her father was *her* husband. She wasn't just filling in for her mother: she was trying to *be* her mother.

But then Sandy's mother came home. Sandy was

happy to see her, but inside she felt nervous without knowing why. When her mother told her she had done a good job of keeping house, Sandy felt embarrassed. She felt as if she had done a very bad job, even though she knew that wasn't true.

After that, Sandy became even more nervous. She began to be afraid of strangers. It seemed to her that someone would try to harm her.

Whenever she saw a stranger she wondered if he were a kidnapper, just waiting to hurt her.

Since no stranger had ever hurt Sandy, why did she suddenly decide that strangers were "after her?" Actually Sandy wasn't afraid of strangers at all. She was really afraid of her hidden wish to grow up.

While her mother was away, Sandy had taken her place. She had enjoyed being treated like an adult. She liked the extra attention and responsibility.

But Sandy was getting this attention only because she was filling in for her mother. To make it permanent, she would have had to grow up and marry her father. And she would have had to make sure her mother didn't come home. The house couldn't have *two* mothers.

Sandy really wanted to grow up and take her mother's place. But she was also afraid and ashamed. What would her mother do if she knew Sandy wanted to get rid of her. "So you want to kick me out," Sandy imagined her mother saying. "Well, you're not a grown woman. You're just a little girl. And *I* can kick *you* out."

These ideas terrified Sandy, so she stopped thinking about them. She "forgot" they were in her mind. But she still felt she was very bad and that something terrible was going to happen to her. She felt as though she *deserved* to be punished. In Sandy's mind the people who were going to carry out the punishment were kidnappers. They were going to take her away from her home.

Luckily, Sandy's parents suspected the real cause of Sandy's uneasiness. They didn't realize how much she wanted to grow up. But they knew it wasn't easy for Sandy to give up being in charge of the house. So they talked to Sandy and encouraged her to tell them about her feelings.

Finally Sandy understood that she was afraid because she was ashamed. She told her parents that she had read a book on how children are born. She admitted how ashamed she felt.

"There's nothing wrong with wondering about sex and babies," her parents said. "If you have any more questions, ask us. We'll be glad to tell you. After all, when you're grown up, you'll probably have a family of your own. You should know the facts."

So Sandy realized she was not an awful person for wanting her own family. Someday she could have one. She didn't have to take away her mother's.

Sandy found out something else too. Because she had had to do so many things on her own, she *had* grown up a bit while her mother was gone. Of course she wasn't as grown up as she would have liked to be. But she felt she deserved more freedom. She wanted to be treated more like an adult. Her parents agreed and Sandy did get something out of substituting for her mother after all.

So, people are usually afraid of strangers because strangers remind them of feelings that they want to hide. There is, however, another reason for this fear of strangers.

Adults often warn children against kidnappers and other strangers with bad intentions. Some adults overdo these warnings until children are afraid of *all* strangers —even those who couldn't possibly hurt them.

Tom, for instance, was petrified with fright every year when school began. After a few months, he would relax and begin to show interest in his classes. His parents couldn't figure out why he never did well at the beginning of the school year. They didn't know that he was afraid—afraid of having a new teacher, afraid of his new classmates. . . .

When Tom was very small his mother had told him in many different ways to beware of strangers. "Never make friends with a stranger," she would say, "unless your father and I tell you it's all right. Never get into a car with a stranger, and if one wants to talk to you, run away." She was afraid of strangers herself. Her parents had told her the same things about strangers when she was small.

Tom's fear of strangers was so overdone that he couldn't even warm up to a new teacher and classmates.

George, who was about Tom's age, had a similar problem. He thought—and often said—that he didn't want friends. When a classmate tried to become friendly, George would start a quarrel or just walk away. He, too, had been warned about strangers.

George really wanted friends. But his parents had warned him to trust no one but his family, who loved him. So George actually felt guilty about wanting friends. He felt as if getting to know and making friends with strangers would be disobeying his parents.

Neither George nor Tom would have had to be scared if they had known *which* strangers to accept—

and which to avoid. Some strangers help us and even protect our lives. Policemen, firemen, dentists, and doctors are all strangers who are trained to help people. You can trust them even if you've never seen them before.

Policemen, for instance, are hired by the community to protect everyone in that community. Their job is to prevent crimes and keep people safe. Still, many children learn to fear and distrust the police. They may hear adults complaining about a traffic ticket "some rotten cop" gave them. This may make the children think that adults don't like the police. But usually this isn't the case. An adult who gets a traffic ticket is angry with himself—he broke the law and got caught. Instead of being mad at himself, it's easier to blame someone else—just as you might kick a door after you've mashed your finger in it. It's not the door's fault but you get angry with the door anyway.

Doctors and dentists, even if they hurt us, are also friends. You make the doctor's job easier if you trust and accept him, and follow his advice. It makes no sense to go to a doctor for advice, and then be afraid to accept it.

Other people, like custodians at school, salesgirls in stores, waitresses, bus drivers, and librarians are also supposed to help us. Many children are afraid of them, imagining that they will scold or make fun of children. But there is no reason to be afraid. If you ask them for help they usually give it.

What strangers should you avoid?

There is usually no reason to distrust a stranger who stops you on the street and asks directions. But there *are* people who approach children in public places, like

27

parks, theaters, or schoolyards, and try to become friendly for *no known reason*.

You should politely avoid these strangers. If they offer you a ride or candy, there is nothing wrong with saying, "No, thank you," and walking away. You aren't being mean. You're being cautious.

You have probably heard stories of strangers who "take children away" and "do terrible things." These stories are often exaggerated. Most adults who approach children for no known reason are unpleasant but not dangerous.

Often they are grownups who are ashamed of their own curiosity about sex. Because they were not permitted to express this curiosity as children, they have never outgrown it. They like to look at or touch the bodies of strange childen. Or they might want to show off their own bodies. But usually they don't do any harm.

Becky, for instance, was five years old when a strange man came up to her in the park. He started talking to her for no known reason. Then he took her behind a bush and told her to pull down her pants. Becky started to pull them down but then she got frightened. "I don't want to," she said and she ran all the way home. The man didn't try to follow her.

Becky's parents were calm when she told them what had happened. They explained that she had nothing to be afraid of, since the man had not hurt her. But she shouldn't go anywhere with a stranger.

This, of course, is not the same thing as accepting help from a stranger if you are hurt or lost. In this case, *there is a known reason* for the stranger's concern. When there is no policeman or other public servant around, a stranger who offers help is putting himself in their place, doing their job of helping you.

It would be a cold world indeed if we could not accept a genuine act of kindness when in need—just because this kindness was offered by a stranger.

CHAPTER FOUR

FEAR OF AUTHORITY AND PUNISHMENT

Authority is the power to give orders—and to make people obey them. Parents, teachers, principals, the police, all have authority. So does the boss in an office or factory. And so do government officials, like the President or the governor of your state.

People in authority are supposed to help you out. They can answer your questions. They can make plans to help people work together. And they can protect you if someone is trying to hurt you.

For instance, if someone steals your ball on the playground, you don't *have to* fight him. What if he's bigger than you? Instead, you tell your teacher. She

30

has the authority to make the person give you back your ball. If he won't give it back, she can take the ball away and punish him.

So, people in authority can help you. But if you do something wrong, they can punish you, too.

Everyone does something wrong now and then. So everyone worries a little about being punished. When you see a person in authority, you sometimes remember the "bad" things you have thought or done. What would the person in authority do if *he* knew about them? This thought might frighten you for a while.

For example, if the teacher comes up while you're playing in the yard, you quiet down. So does everyone else. Your game may not be very noisy, but you worry a little anyway.

If the teacher looks at you in class, you sometimes feel funny. Why is she looking at you? Have you done something wrong? Is she going to ask you a question?

Adults worry about authority too. In an office, everyone works harder when the boss walks by. Traffic on the highway slows down whenever a policeman appears.

But some people seem terrified of authority. They never stop worrying that they will be punished. They are afraid to talk to anyone in authority. They are like a person who, instead of slowing down when he sees a policeman, stops his car in the middle of the road and gets out with his hands over his head.

People who act this way aren't really afraid of authority. They are afraid of *their own feelings about authority*. Like Caroline and Grace and Roger, they don't want to think they have strong, violent feelings. They prefer to think they are afraid of authority itself. Frank's case is a good example.

31

Frank was in the seventh grade. He was a shy person and small for his age. One day at school Frank accidently ran into Harold, a boy he didn't know very well. Harold tripped and twisted his arm.

"What do you mean, running into me?" yelled Harold. He was mad because his arm hurt.

"I'm sorry," said Frank in a small voice.

"Look where you're going," snapped Harold and then he walked away.

After that Harold decided to be mean to Frank. Harold was a very angry person. He got into fights all the time. And he was mean to Frank because he felt that Frank had tripped him on purpose.

Sometimes Harold made faces at Frank. Sometimes he waved his hands at Frank as if he were going to hit him. When they were playing on the schoolyard, Harold often ran into Frank and knocked him down. And several times Harold and his friends waited for Frank after school and threw rocks at him.

Frank couldn't fight Harold by himself. Harold was just too big and angry. But he didn't ask for help from his parents, his teachers, or the principal. He just let Harold make him miserable.

Why? Because Frank didn't believe that people in authority would help him. He thought they would just get mad at him. "What did you do to Harold to make him angry with you?" Frank imagined his teachers asking. "If he hates you, it must be because you deserve it."

Frank really felt he *did* deserve Harold's bullying. He never actually said, "I deserve it." But for some reason, it seemed right.

How could Harold's bullying seem right to Frank? And why was he afraid that people in authority would punish him instead of helping him? The answer lies in Frank's deepest feelings.

Frank felt bad about himself all the time. He felt like a bad person. He didn't know why he felt this way. But whenever anything bad happened to him, he blamed himself.

Frank didn't understand that he felt bad about himself because he too was an angry person. Inside, he was just as angry as Harold was. But Frank believed that anger was wrong. He was terribly ashamed of himself for feeling any anger.

This shame had started when Frank was very young. He had a little sister who was very sick when she was born. Frank had been furious. His sister took up all his mother's time. It had seemed as if he never saw his mother any more.

Sometimes Frank had wanted to jump up and down and scream in his baby sister's room. Sometimes he had run noisily past her door. "Be quiet," Frank's mother would tell him. "You know she's sick. You mustn't disturb her or she'll get worse."

"I wish she *would* get worse," Frank thought. Then he had felt ashamed. What if, just by wishing, he *could* make his sister sicker? What if she died because he made too much noise? Frank became terrified of his angry feelings. They seemed powerful enough to kill.

After that, Frank never made much noise in the house. He didn't slam doors or throw toys. He never raised his voice. He stopped showing his anger in any way.

But since anger doesn't just go away, Frank didn't stop being angry with his sister. He simply decided it wasn't safe to be angry with her—or anyone else. What

33

if he killed someone by mistake? So instead of being angry with other people, Frank became angry with himself.

He punished himself a lot. He lost things he needed, like his homework, or his gloves or his lunch. He was continually telling himself how stupid and worthless he was. He hated himself so much, he imagined that everyone else hated him too. He thought his classmates, his parents, his teachers and the principal were all waiting to tease or punish him.

That was why Frank didn't go to the principal about Harold. He imagined the principal knew how "bad" he was—just as he thought Harold knew. And so Frank suffered a whole year of Harold's bullying. Because he was afraid to ask for help from authority, he threw away his only chance to fight Harold.

The next year Harold moved away. But other people frightened Frank just as much as Harold had. Usually he was afraid of people who weren't even mad at him. But he was just as afraid of his teachers or the principal so he never asked them for help.

Not everyone who is afraid of authority *seems* to be as afraid as Frank was. Denise, for instance, didn't seem to be afraid of her teacher at all. But she was just as afraid as Frank.

Denise was a very bright girl. She had read a lot. She always answered questions in class. She seemed very confident. But she had one problem: she was careless.

Half the time Denise didn't finish her homework. Her desk was a mess. If the teacher passed out papers for the class to keep, Denise lost them. She was always leaving her books, pencils, and crayons at home.

Denise said these things weren't important. "It doesn't

matter if I bring my book if I know my work," she would say. And she usually knew her work because she had an excellent memory.

Inside, though, Denise worried about being careless. No one else in her class was that careless. What was wrong with her?

The answer is that Denise was careless because she was afraid. She was always afraid that her teacher would criticize her.

You might think, "Of course the teacher would criticize her if she was careless." But Denise was afraid she'd be criticized *whether she was careless or not.*

Denise's fear, like Frank's, had started when she was very small. She had an older brother and two older sisters. They were all allowed to do things Denise couldn't do. They could go to bed later than she could. They could go to school or to their friends' houses by themselves. They had their own crayons and colored pencils and many other things—and they wouldn't let Denise use any of them.

This situation made Denise very angry. She didn't understand that she would be allowed to do the things her brother and sisters could do—when she got old enough. She wanted to do them right now!

But Denise wasn't big or strong enough to do the things her brother and sisters did. She tried to ride their bicycle, but she couldn't push the pedals. When she tried to color, she couldn't make neat lines, the way her brother and sisters could. She could only scribble. And once, when she tried to go somewhere by herself, she got lost.

"You see," her brother and sisters said, "you can't do what we do. You're too little." Sometimes they laughed at Denise, and that made her angrier than ever.

As Denise got older, she learned to do more. But her brother and sisters got older too. They could always do more things than Denise. So, instead of feeling better, she kept on feeling angry.

Like Roger and Frank, Denise didn't want to believe she was angry. So she projected her anger. She thought that people older than she was—her brother and sisters, her teachers, the principal—were angry with *her*.

"They all hate me," she thought. "They all think I'm stupid. And they'll say *everything* I do is stupid, no matter what I do."

That was why Denise was so careless. She was sure her teacher would criticize her no matter what she did. So she didn't dare work hard on anything. If the teacher criticized something Denise was proud of, Denise would feel terrible. Being careless was safer. If the teacher didn't like what she'd done, Denise could say, "Well, I didn't work on it anyway."

You can see that Denise's problem was much like Frank's. They were both angry and they projected their anger. They both believed it was *other* people who were angry with *them*. So they were afraid of punishment.

Denise and Frank felt that people in authority were always watching them. They thought of their teachers as strict and powerful. And since they felt bad about themselves to begin with, they were sure they could never be perfect enough to please people in authority.

Other people are afraid of authority for a different reason. They imagine that people in authority don't care about them. Or they worry that their parents and teachers don't really have any power at all.

For instance, a person with this kind of fear might be afraid to ask a teacher for help. If someone stole his ball on the playground, he might think about telling a teacher. But he would imagine her answering, "Why are you telling me? If your want your ball back, it's up to you to get it."

If this really happened you would feel very frightened. You might just leave the ball with the bully who took it. And suppose *no one* in authority would help or protect you? In school, you'd never learn much. The teachers wouldn't show you how to do hard arithmetic problems or spell long words. People could steal your things without being punished. Burglars could break into your house and the police would ignore it.

All this would make you furious. "You're supposed to be in authority!" you would tell your teacher, and the others. "Why don't you do your job and *help* me?"

And some people really *do* feel like that. They feel that no one in authority will help them. They think there is no one to protect them. And they are afraid that no one in authority will tell them what is allowed and what is not allowed. Then they won't even know how to stay out of trouble.

Harold, the bully in Frank's story, had exactly this problem. He felt that no one in authority would stand up for him. This made him angry. And because he felt so helpless and angry, he was desperate to make *anyone* in authority help him—or even notice him.

When Harold was five, his parents were divorced. His father moved to the other side of town. Harold went to live half the time with him and half the time with his mother, and this change really upset him.

He couldn't understand what was going on. Why did

his father go away? Did his parents love him? Maybe they didn't. Maybe they got divorced so that each one would have to take care of him only half of the time.

Harold really worried about this. What if his parents stopped taking care of him? It did seem that since the divorce they had less time to spend with him. And each of them made different rules for him. His mother made him go to bed at nine o'clock. His father didn't seem to care. His father wanted him to play football. His mother thought football was a violent, boring game. Harold felt abandoned and confused.

Harold was so worried that he started to do bad things just for attention. Even if his parents were spanking him, at least they were *there*. They were talking to him and thinking about him. And they were telling him what they didn't want him to do.

But Harold was still confused. He knew a few things his parents didn't like. But he didn't know whether to believe people when they said something was right or wrong. Did his parents make rules because they cared about him and they wanted him to be safe and happy? Or did they make rules just to shut him up? Just to keep him out of their way? Harold didn't know, and doing mean things was the only way to make sure he would be noticed—or so he thought.

So Harold got into a lot of trouble. He started fights and hurt people. He disobeyed teachers. He broke things. When Harold did something bad, he felt safe. He knew he would be punished. That he could count on. So he didn't feel so confused and lonely and help-less.

Frank, Denise, and Harold all had mistaken ideas about people in authority. Denise and Frank thought people in authority hated them. Harold thought authority wouldn't help him. And all these ideas really came from the feelings Denise, Frank, and Harold were hiding from themselves.

If you are afraid of authority, you are also probably worried about your own feelings. But if you really believe that your parents or teachers are too vague about rules, or too strict, you may be able to help yourself.

If you feel lost, like Harold, you may be able to find out some rules just by asking. Ask your parents, "What may I do? What won't you allow me to do?" If you're mad at them, tell them what made you mad and why. And if this doesn't help, try talking to your teachers or school counselor. They can help teach you what things are likely to get you in trouble, and what things aren't.

Suppose you are afraid, like Frank and Denise, that you'll never be able to live up to the rules. In this case, your problem is different. How many rules are "too many"? What is a "fair rule"? There is no perfect way to decide. Which is a fairer bedtime, nine o'clock or nine-thirty? Most questions about rules are like asking whether red or blue is a prettier color. The answer isn't in a book; no one can tell you an answer. The answer depends entirely on which color *you* like better.

There is one good way to decide whether rules are too strict. Ask yourself how you feel about the rules. Do they make you feel uneasy, frightened, or confined? This is not the same as being angry because a rule keeps you from getting something you want. A child who has to follow too many rules often feels cramped and tense. He feels that nothing he does is right.

If you feel you are being punished unfairly, try to

39

persuade your mother, father, or teacher—whoever is in charge—that you meant no harm and feel you had a *right* to do what you did. If this gets you nowhere, talk to another adult who will understand, and maybe offer you some suggestions.

If your mother, for instance, is too strict, go directly to her to talk things over. If this doesn't work, talk things over with your father. Then all three of you can sit down and discuss what's going on.

Many times an adult is too strict because *he* is unhappy or nervous. He may be worried about problems of his own. Sometimes he may punish you by mistake for breaking a rule you didn't understand. Or sometimes he might be mad because he is in a bad mood, and you are bothering him—maybe making too much noise. Adults are people and have their bad days just as you do. They also have problems of their own to worry them.

If your parents seem too strict, talk to them about it. That way, you can find out what is going on with them. You shouldn't feel shy about asking. After all, it is your family too. You have a right to know about the things that affect it—and you. Besides, if you know what your parents are feeling, it's easier to make them understand how *you* feel.

All this goes for other people in authority, too. Like your parents, they are human. You can talk to them. If you are afraid of authority, you lose the chance for a great deal of help. People in authority aren't your enemies. Like anyone else, they can become your friends.

CHAPTER FIVE

FEAR OF SCHOOL

"Fear of school" sounds like something that happens on the first day of school. You probably remember feeling worried when you first went to kindergarten. Or if you didn't, you can remember children who cried as their mothers left them at school. You may even remember one or two who got sick and had to go home.

Many children are afraid of school, at first, and that makes sense. After all, what do you know about school before you go? Not much. It's new and strange—and it changes your whole life.

Once you go to school, though, you find out there's

nothing to be afraid of. School is just another thing you learn to do, like bike riding. Bike riding can be frightening, too, at first. But once you learn to keep your balance, you can do it without even thinking. School is the same way.

At least most children get used to school. But some don't. Some who are not afraid in the beginning, become afraid later on. And some who are afraid, don't realize they are. They just feel tense when they're at school. Or maybe they get headaches or stomachaches when they have to leave for school. Or maybe they worry about what's going on at home while they're in school.

If you're afraid of school, you might get sick a lot. This is pretty common. In fact fear of school is so common, psychiatrists have a special name for it—*school phobia*.

How can you make yourself sick? Well, you're using energy when you're worrying about school. Your muscles get tight. You fidget. If you get too worn out from worrying, you're more likely to get sick. Just as you're more likely to get sick if you don't get enough sleep.

So fear of school can be a pretty serious problem. To overcome it, a person has to find out why he's afraid.

We know that many fears are caused by feelings we're afraid to admit. What feelings do you think of when you think about school?

To start with, being in school means you're not at home. Usually that doesn't bother you. But suppose for some reason you're afraid to leave home? Then, of course, you'd be afraid to go to school.

Think about it this way. Fear of school is much like

fear of the dark. When you're off by yourself, in school or alone in your room at night, your parents aren't there. And, if you feel lonely and helpless, if you feel your parents won't take care of you, you are terrified whenever you have to go away. What if they aren't there when you get back?

This is called fear of abandonment and fear of abandonment causes most fear of school. Priscilla's case is a good example.

Priscilla was very shy in school. When she was asked a question in class, she answered so softly that no one could hear. She sat very straight in her seat and looked around as if she were afraid something would attack her.

Priscilla worried all day. She didn't know exactly what she worried about. But she didn't feel *safe*. Sometimes she was afraid she would get lost at school. She had dreams about getting lost there, too. In her dreams she would ask directions but no one would tell her where to go.

One year Priscilla's class went for a field trip to the airport. Priscilla got lost in the huge terminal. She followed corridor after corridor, but she was as lost as ever. Finally her teacher found her. But Priscilla was so afraid she wasn't able to go on with the tour. She had to be sent home.

Priscilla's teacher, Mrs. Sanchez, thought a lot about what had happened to Priscilla. Why had the girl been so frightened at the airport? Why did she look nervous and unhappy all the time? One afternoon Mrs. Sanchez went to visit Priscilla's parents.

Priscilla's mother was home. She invited Mrs. Sanchez to sit down. "What's the problem?" she asked.

Mrs. Sanchez started to explain. Then, from down the hall came the sound of a baby howling. "I'm sorry," said Priscilla's mother. "Just a minute."

But it wasn't just a minute. As soon as the mother came back, Priscilla's little brother ran in. "Phil won't give me my plane!"

Another brother appeared in the doorway. "It's not his. I traded it to him for a tank and he never gave me one."

"Will you kids get out of here?" Priscilla's mother ordered. "We've got company!"

But every few minutes one of Priscilla's brothers or sisters came back. The littlest sister wanted to show her mother a rock. Priscilla's brothers started fighting in their bedroom. The baby wouldn't keep quiet. Janet, Priscilla's oldest sister, came to ask for lunch money.

When Mrs. Sanchez left, she thought she understood Priscilla's problem a little more. You can see, as she did, why Priscilla might have been nervous. She hardly got any attention from her mother. None of her brothers and sisters did either. There were so many of them that they always had to be fighting for their mother's attention.

Because of this problem, Priscilla didn't like to go to school. When she was gone, the younger children could be with her mother all day. Priscilla felt left out when she was in school. She felt as if she'd been thrown out of the house. It seemed no one loved her very much.

That was why Priscilla was afraid of being lost. Inside, she felt lost all the time. Being reminded of that helpless, lonely feeling terrified her.

Mrs. Sanchez understood some of Priscilla's feelings.

She had known other children like Priscilla. So she encouraged the girl to feel relaxed and open. She smiled at her sometimes. If she met Priscilla at recess, she would say something friendly.

Slowly Priscilla realized what Mrs. Sanchez was trying to tell her. She was saying, "If you need help, I'll help you." Mrs. Sanchez couldn't just walk up and *say* this. Priscilla wouldn't have had any way to believe her. But, by *being* friendly for several weeks, Mrs. Sanchez let Priscilla know that she really liked her.

So Priscilla decided to trust Mrs. Sanchez. They became friends. After that, Priscilla wasn't as frightened of school. She knew there was someone there she could count on. That helped her get over the fact that her mother couldn't be with her as much as Priscilla would have liked.

Priscilla's problem happens to many children. It happens if you are afraid you will have to be away from your mother for a long time. You may feel left out because you have a large family, like Priscilla's. Or you may feel afraid because your mother is working or because she has many other things on her mind. No matter why you feel you're going to lose your mother, it worries you a lot—so much that you don't want to leave her at all, especially to go to school.

School may also frighten you for other reasons. For instance, you may not like one of your teachers.

There are many reasons you might not like someone. But many times you "hate him at first sight." You can't understand why you don't like him. Everything he does just makes you mad.

How can you hate someone you don't even know?

Many times, you only *think* you don't like him. He reminds you of someone else—someone you *do* know. Someone who really makes you mad.

The person who makes you mad is closer to you than your teacher is. You don't want to tell him you're mad, because you are afraid to hurt him. So it's safer to be mad at someone who only *reminds* you of him. Take the case of Jack.

When school started, Jack had a new teacher, Mrs. Cooper. She had never been at his school before. Mrs. Cooper made her class do lots of homework. If any of her students talked in class, she sent them out of the room right away. Everyone decided she was very strict.

Jack started hating his teacher the first day he saw her. He hated her voice. "It's dried-up and mean," he thought. He hated her name and the way she looked and everything else about her.

After a while the class stopped being scared of Mrs. Cooper. They knew what she wanted them to do and got used to it. But Jack felt as scared and mad at her as ever. At night, he'd dread the thought of going back to school. "I'll have to see her ugly face again," he thought.

All day Jack was miserable in school. He didn't have any fun playing at recess. His work seemed twice as hard as it ever had. He seemed to hear his teacher's voice droning in his ears, bossing him around and criticizing him.

One day Jack didn't know the answer on a test. He copied someone else's answer. Mrs. Cooper saw him cheating and kept him after school.

"Why did you cheat?" she asked him.

"Because—" Jack was so scared he said the first thing

that came into his head. "Because I don't like you! That's why!"

As Jack heard himself say the words his stomach sank. Now he was really in for it.

"Just why don't you like me?" asked Mrs. Cooper crossly.

"Because—"

But what could Jack say? "Because you have a mean voice?" "Because you have a funny name?" "Because you're making me stay after school for cheating?"

Jack realized these weren't such good reasons for hating someone. He wondered why he *did* hate Mrs. Cooper.

"I don't know," he answered her. "I—I guess we just don't get along."

"Do you think I'm too strict?"

Jack wanted to say yes. But he knew nobody else thought she was *that* strict. He felt puzzled and frightened.

"No," he said. "I don't know why."

"Don't be afraid," said Mrs. Cooper. "I'm not going to punish you for saying you don't like me. But, you are going to have to do an extra assignment because you cheated. That way you'll know your work and you won't be tempted to copy someone else's."

When Jack got home, he felt better. He felt Mrs. Cooper had been fair with him. He sat in his room and wondered why she bothered him so much.

As he sat there, he heard his mother's voice. She was talking to his sister. Suddenly Jack realized that Mrs. Cooper's voice reminded him of his mother's. It sounded strict and mean, just like his mother's.

"That's weird," thought Jack. "Maybe I'm really mad

at my mother. After all, Mrs. Cooper never did anything to me. But her voice sounds just like Mom's when she's bawling me out."

Jack was right. He *was* mad at his mother. And after that, Jack wasn't quite as scared of Mrs. Cooper. He still didn't like her very much. But he realized she wasn't the same as his mother. And, little by little, he began to learn more about Mrs. Cooper. He found that she was pretty strict, but usually fair. And if he ever needed help with his lessons, she'd help him until he understood.

Jack was still angry with his mother. But instead of taking it out on Mrs. Cooper, he began to think about why his mother made him so angry and what he could do to change these things. Could he talk to her about the way he felt? Could he change some of the things *he* was doing that made *her* angry? These were definite possibilities and Jack was on his way to solving his problems with his mother.

But parents aren't the only people who can make you angry. And teachers aren't the only ones who can remind you of that anger.

Some people are angry with their brothers and sisters. Now, the other children in school are like your brothers and sisters. The teacher, like your mother, takes care of all of you. So if you are really angry with your brothers and sisters, you may not like going to school. You may not like the other children because they remind you too much of your anger.

Most brothers and sisters do have arguments and fights. They are usually fighting over their parents' love. Sharing that love isn't easy. It's hard to share *anything* you really care about.

48

Some children, though, don't feel they are sharing their parents' love. They feel they aren't getting *anything at all*. Their brothers and sisters seem to get all the presents, all the praise, and all the attention from their parents.

How would you feel in this situation? Mad! And if you were mad enough, you might be afraid to be around your brothers and sisters—or anyone who reminded you of them. You'd be afraid of the angry things you'd do and say—and afraid of being punished. For instance, let's look at the case of Jeff.

Jeff didn't like school. He had a strange problem there. If he had to stay in class too long, he felt as if he were choking. It always seemed as if he wouldn't be able to breathe for another minute. When recess came, Jeff made for the door like someone running for his life.

That was the only time Jeff ever moved fast. Everyone called him "lazy." He never worked hard. He never even played games during noon hour. He always felt a little tired, and he got sick a lot.

Why was Jeff tired? Because he was using all his energy worrying. He really worried every second he was in school. The only time he ever felt good was when he was off by himself, without another person in sight.

Naturally, Jeff's grades weren't very good. His parents didn't get mad at him, though. They said Jeff's brother, Rick, was already smart enough for both of them.

Rick was in high school. He was a straight-A student. Every year he came home with several awards. His parents, who had never won any prizes or done anything special, were proud of him. His mother even got a job to earn the money to send him to college.

Rick wasn't a bad brother as brothers go. He let Jeff use his things. He never told Jeff to go away when his friends came to see him. So, part of Jeff really liked Rick. But the other part couldn't stand him.

Jeff was always fighting with himself, inside.

"I hate you!" he wanted to tell Rick. "Mom and Dad think you're so great! You get everything and I don't get anything! It's not fair!"

"Oh, no," he'd answer himself. "You can't say *that* to Rick! He'd get mad, and Mom and Dad would be on his side. They'd never even speak to you again. Besides, it's not Rick's fault that he was born smart and you're a dummy."

But Jeff couldn't stop being angry with Rick. He was so angry that, at the back of his mind, he always wanted to take his anger out on someone. He was afraid to play games with other children because he feared he would knock someone down or kick him. And he was afraid to be in class, so close to other people, because he really wanted to hurt them.

That was why he felt as if he were choking in class. Have you ever heard the expression "choking with rage"? People who are very angry often choke and splutter. They try to yell at you, but they are so angry they can't even talk.

This choking is caused by fear. Some people are so afraid to talk about their anger that they choke back their words. Jeff, too, was choking back his words. He was secretly afraid that he would get up in class and start yelling at everybody.

Jeff's problem stayed with him until he was in high school. He finally decided he must be sick if he had trouble breathing, so he went to his doctor. His doctor couldn't find anything wrong with him. But he explained to Jeff that choking often means you are angry.

So Jeff then talked his problem over with the school counselor. He realized how furious Rick made him. Once he was able to tell someone how angry he was with Rick, he didn't have to direct his anger at the other people in his class. He could start working on his relationships at home and stop being afraid of school.

Jeff was very lucky to get over his fear. Like anger, fear—whether it has to do with school or anything else—doesn't just go away. If fear of school isn't overcome, it can go on all your life. It can make you very unhappy in college. And it can carry over into work. At work, you may have to be with many people, as in class. Or you may have to work for a boss as strict as your teachers.

If you think you are afraid of school, you should take the steps we've already mentioned in overcoming fear. Ask yourself some questions. What scares you about school? The teacher? The other children? Do you feel lonely at school?

Let's say you're afraid of your teacher. What frightens you about him or her? Do you feel angry with your teacher? Does he or she remind you of someone you're mad at?

If you just don't know the answers to any of these questions, try talking to someone about them. It should be someone you trust—someone who understands you.

Remember, too, that you are stronger than you think

in dealing with fear. Once you realize you are fighting something inside yourself—your own feelings—you'll be more confident. After all, your feelings aren't stronger or smarter than you are. You created them—and you can control them.

CHAPTER SIX

FEAR OF FAILURE

Sometimes you just *know* you are going to fail. You've had that feeling. Maybe you're up on the diving board with everyone watching you, and you're sure you'll do a belly-flop. Or you're about to take a test and you're really convinced you've failed it. You feel cold and scared. You picture everyone laughing or yelling at you.

Pretty often, these fears don't come true. You dive off the diving board or pass the test. Then you feel very happy that the terrible things you imagined didn't happen.

But sometimes you really do fail. You fail over and over again at the same thing. And every time you fail you feel more frightened of failing again. But somehow you *can't* make yourself succeed.

In fact, your fear makes it even harder to succeed. Sometimes, for instance, you're so frightened of a test that your mind goes blank. Then you can't answer *any* questions, so you don't even have a chance of passing.

How can fear of failure make you fail?

A few years ago a teacher named John Holt examined this question in a book called *How Children Fail*. When he was teaching, he saw that some of his students couldn't stop failing. He would tell these students everything they needed to know to pass his tests. He spent hours trying to teach them arithmetic and spelling and English. Nothing helped: they always failed.

One day Mr. Holt was drilling one of his students for an arithmetic test. The boy sat silent. He just couldn't do the work. Suddenly Mr. Holt asked him, "What are you thinking about?"

The boy shrugged. "I'm thinking about how my father's going to beat me up when I fail the test."

Mr. Holt wondered about this for a long time. "That boy didn't even try to learn the work," he thought. "He *expected* to fail. He was so sure he would fail that you'd think he was *planning* to fail.

"In fact, it must be hard work for these kids not to learn a thing in class every day. It's as if they were *trying* not to learn anything."

Trying not to learn anything? That didn't seem to make much sense. But Mr. Holt watched his class day after day.

He saw that the children who always failed never thought about his questions. They just shouted out anything that sounded like the right answer. Sometimes they gave answers they knew were wrong.

When they gave their answers, they never sounded confident. They sounded shaky. Sometimes they said the answer so fast or so softly no one could hear it. They were *frightened* of something.

Could fear be the reason the children were trying not to learn? Mr. Holt decided it was. He decided that some of his students were trying to fail because they were *afraid to succeed*.

You may say, "That's ridiculous. How could anybody be afraid of success. When you succeed in school, you get good grades. Your parents and teachers are proud of you. You feel good about yourself. There's nothing to be afraid of."

But Mr. Holt discovered that a student who was used to failing couldn't just sit back and enjoy a sudden success. He'd think about the *new* assignments he'd have to do. He'd worry that now he was going to get more and harder work than ever!

New work didn't frighten the students who were used to succeeding. They figured they would do just as well at the new jobs as they had on the old ones. A student who failed had different ideas.

"Think how much trouble the old work was," he'd say to himself. "The new work will be much worse." So he'd fail again. This way he could stay with the work he knew. It was boring but it wasn't new or frightening.

This may sound odd. But think about it this way. When you succeed you learn to do something you've never done before. After that you're not quite the same person. You're a person who knows a little more. You've grown a little, changed a little.

And change isn't always easy to handle. It's hard to know where change stops. "If my mind can grow and change," you might think, "what about my feelings? What if I stop loving the people I love now? What if they change, too, and stop loving me?"

This is a very common fear. You've probably read fairy tales about children who are magically changed into animals. When they try to go home, their parents don't recognize them and chase them away.

To some children, succeeding would be as awful and threatening as being changed into an animal. For instance, a child may have the opportunity to do something or learn something no one in his family can do. He may think his family will be angry with him if he learns this thing. So he won't try. He'll make mistakes. He'll ignore what he's being taught. Finally he'll convince himself that he really couldn't do it in the first place. Then, of course, he'll fail—as Lucy did in the following story.

Lucy couldn't do arithmetic. All the other subjects were easy for her, but when it came to numbers—"Forget it," she'd say sadly.

Forgetting was just Lucy's problem. If the teacher asked Lucy, "How do you add?" Lucy could tell her. She knew *how* to work every kind of problem. She could say her addition and multiplication combinations all the way through without a mistake. But when it came to doing problems on paper, Lucy would always do something wrong. As time went on, she became convinced she couldn't do arithmetic. She hated it and hardly ever studied it.

As you can imagine, Lucy got very discouraged with arithmetic. She asked her older sister Beth to help her, but Beth hated numbers too. "I don't see why they even make you take arithmetic!" Beth complained. "It never makes any sense." That made Lucy feel terrible. She looked up to Beth. If Beth couldn't work with numbers, Lucy was sure she didn't have much chance.

Lucy had more and more trouble with arithmetic. In junior high she couldn't do math. "I've got to do something about this," she decided. "I just can't stand to get one more bad grade!" But Lucy couldn't figure out how to help herself.

Then, that spring, Beth decided to go away to college in the fall. She could have gone to the state university, near home, but she wanted to go to a college far away. This meant she would hardly ever be able to visit her family.

This made Lucy mad at Beth. She felt Beth was deserting her. "You didn't have to go so far away!" Lucy said. "Now I won't be able to visit you! I'll hardly ever see you any more."

"What do you want me to do, hang around here?" yelled Beth. "I'm supposed to make up my mind what I want to do. So stop acting like a three-year-old!"

That night Lucy cried. She had never felt so angry with Beth before.

Two days later, Lucy and Beth still hadn't really made up. Lucy wouldn't talk to Beth. She sat silently in their room, studying for her math test the next day.

When the test came back, Lucy got a surprise. She

had done well! No stupid mistakes. She'd missed several problems, but not nearly as many as usual.

On the next test, though, Lucy did as badly as ever.

Lucy was mystified. She went to talk to her school counselor.

"How could I suddenly do well, and then do badly again?" she asked.

"Did you study more for the first test?" inquired the counselor.

"Well . . . maybe a little. I was studying all alone. My sister and I usually study together, but that night we had a fight."

"How do you feel about your sister?" the counselor asked.

So Lucy told him how close she was to Beth, and why they'd had a fight.

"I've got an idea," said the counselor. "It's really just a guess, because I don't know your sister. But think about it. You love your sister. Now she's done something really mean to you. She's going away. Don't you want to get back at her?"

"I guess so," said Lucy. "But I don't want to really hurt her."

"Of course not. So hitting her or ruining her things is out. What else can you do to make her feel bad?"

"Not talk to her. Just sit with my nose in a book all the time."

"Studying. And what were you studying?"

"Math."

He nodded. "Right. Math. Something Beth can't do."

"You mean," said Lucy, "I was trying to show Beth up by studying math?"

"I think it's a pretty safe bet. You must have read

the book more carefully and thought more about the problems than usual. That's why you did better on the test."

Lucy sat for a while and thought. "You know," she said finally, "I have an idea. You say I was trying to show Beth up by studying harder and doing better."

He nodded.

"Maybe I do badly the rest of the time because I'm trying *not* to show Beth up."

"Why do you think that?"

"Well—I've never wanted to be away from Beth in anything. When I was little, I played with all her dolls. I wouldn't let anybody buy me any others. I liked all the foods she liked. I told her all my secrets and she told me hers. It was always like that until now."

"So you hated math because she did?"

"Well, maybe I mean . . . isn't it harder to do well at something you hate?"

"Not only that. You can forget things on purpose, you know. That's why studying wasn't much help to you. At the bottom, you were afraid to learn math. So of course you forgot what you learned."

Lucy realized that her counselor was right.

She remembered how strange and new arithmetic had seemed to her when she'd first learned it. It was outside the world she knew. Beth couldn't help her with it. By learning arithmetic well, Lucy would be *leaving* Beth—just as Beth was leaving her to go to college.

So, failure at math seemed like the way to stay close to Beth. Success would have made Lucy feel lonely and unsure.

Lucy was shocked to realize that she wanted to fail. "How can I knock some sense into my head?" she wondered. "It's stupid to think learning math will take me away from Beth!"

That night Beth came up to Lucy. "Are you still mad at me?" she asked.

"No," said Lucy. "I want to tell you something."

She told Beth what she'd learned about her wish to fail.

Beth and Lucy talked a long time that night. Afterwards, Lucy felt better. She realized she and Beth would still be close to each other even if they both learned new things and saw new places.

So Lucy studied math again. Beth encouraged her. Lucy didn't learn everything about math right away. But she did better and better. And by the next year Lucy was starting to get the grades she'd wanted.

Lucy conquered her fear of new and strange things. You can see how learning math was frightening for her. It seemed to take her away from Beth. But learning math isn't the only kind of success that can seem frightening.

Making friends and letting other people like you is a kind of success. Everyone wants to find someone to like, someone who can help him and keep him company. If you haven't any friends, you feel you've failed somehow.

If you're not confident, though, you may try *not* to make friends. You feel safer without friends. You're used to being alone. If you had friends, you wouldn't know what to say to them. You'd have to be afraid of losing them.

You may not realize you're trying to keep from making friends. But, just as Lucy was forgetting her arithmetic because she wanted to fail, you are staying away from people. Your words and actions say, "I want to be alone. I don't need you."

How can that happen? Let's look at the case of Joyce.

Joyce was always acting silly. She laughed at nothing at all. When her teacher asked her questions in class, she gave stupid answers. And when the other kids tried to talk to her, Joyce would say silly, meaningless things to them.

You can see that it would have been hard to get to know Joyce. She was never serious. You couldn't find out anything about her because she never gave straight answers. And she seemed pretty ridiculous, too.

Joyce acted silly because she was afraid. Just as Lucy was afraid to learn arithmetic, Joyce was afraid to make friends. Neither girl wanted to grow or change. Like Lucy, too, Joyce was close to her family. She was afraid of anything that might make her different from them.

Joyce couldn't really share a friend with her mother and father. She had to separate herself from them to go out and play with people her own age. So she kept on acting silly.

If Joyce could have realized that she could love her family even if she did new things, she would have been a lot happier. Because she was afraid to make friends, she was lonely. She could have enjoyed other people if she'd overcome her fear. And they would have enjoyed being with her, too.

This is something to remember if you are having a hard time succeeding. The odds are a hundred to one that you *can* do the thing that's giving you trouble.

Why? Well, first, everything seems harder when you've never done it before. Think about the skills you've already learned: reading, writing, counting, swimming, bicycling, jumping rope . . . remember how hard they seemed when you couldn't do them? Think how easy they really are. It was your fear of something new and strange that made them seem hard.

Secondly, the things that you can't do now are the ones you're most afraid of. Otherwise you would have learned them already. So, if you fail at all, it's because you're fighting your fears of these things.

Finally, most of the things you need to learn just aren't that hard to learn. School, for instance, is set up to give *all* children an education. If your teachers gave everyone work too hard to do, no one would learn anything. So you are *supposed* to be able to do your schoolwork. It is planned that way.

The same thing is true of making friends. You may be secretly afraid that you aren't as smart or good-looking as other people. That is really just your fear talking. Try to remember all the bad things you think about yourself when you're feeling unhappy. Could anyone *really* be that bad? And how do you know all these things are true? You probably have no real reason to believe them. They're just good excuses for you to keep from having the friends you want—because you're afraid to succeed.

So, if you fail over and over, ask yourself if you really want to succeed. What might happen if you succeed? Something frightening? If you can answer these questions, you can clear your mind of fear. Then you will be free—not just to succeed, but to enjoy what you're doing as well.

CHAPTER SEVEN

FEAR OF BEING DIFFERENT

"Nobody understands me."

Everyone feels this way sometimes. You don't seem to be able to get through to anyone. You tell someone something and it just doesn't seem to register.

This is not an easy situation. But imagine what it would be like if you felt you couldn't ever communicate. You'd feel permanently left out. It might seem you were a stranger in your own family, or else someone from another planet.

Do you feel as though you're odd? Different from other people? Many children do. And it frightens them.

If you feel you're a "different kind of person" then you probably feel that there's no reason for other people to like you. You're completely alone—as though you're the only person on earth who speaks your language. You probably feel as though you can't learn "their" language. You're too different.

"Oh, come on," you might tell yourself. "How am I different? I have arms and legs and a body and a head like everyone else. I can talk. I was born. I had a mother and father. *How* am I different?"

You might answer yourself, "I'm just different."

But the real question is, different from what?

Since you're not different from other people, you must be different from something else. Could you be different from what *you* think you ought to be?

After all, you learn how you're "supposed" to be by watching the people around you, especially your family. It's by the way they act and talk and dress that you get your idea of how you are supposed to act and talk and dress.

For instance, if your parents are very friendly and have a lot of guests in your home, you'll decide people should be friendly. You'll find it quite natural when someone invites you to his house. If your parents hardly ever have anyone over, you'll decide people don't visit each other very much.

Little by little, from watching your parents, your older brothers and sisters, and any older people who live with you—like your grandparents—you get an idea of the way you are supposed to be. It is like a picture of yourself inside your head. Another name for it is an "image."

When you have to decide whether or not to do something, you look at your image. You say to yourself, "Is this what I'm supposed to do? Is this right?" You may do things you've been *told* not to do, but you hardly ever do anything that doesn't go with your image of yourself.

For instance, if you think of yourself as a quiet, shy, polite person, you probably won't yell at other people or hit them, even if you get mad. You may do other "wrong" things, like not finishing your homework, but you won't do things that a quiet, shy, polite person wouldn't do.

And the real problems start when your image of yourself is something the real you *can't* be. If you feel "different," "not made the right way," "out of place," or "weird," you are probably trying to be something you can't be. And the only thing to do is to find out what that something is.

So—what is it? It's probably something you learned by observing your parents.

For instance, you might have decided, when you were very young, that it wasn't enough to imitate your parents. You might have wanted to *be* just like them. Exactly like them—even though that's impossible. After all, your parents were grownup, and no matter how hard you try, *you* just can't grow up all at once.

At times it probably bothers you not to be grownup. Adults seem to be able to do everything so easily. They can hammer nails without hitting their fingers. They can read without stumbling over the words or asking, "What does that mean?" They can beat you at games. So if you think you should be able to do everything as well as an adult, right *now*, you can get very frustrated. And if you feel you *have* to do things that well, you'll become desperate—even frightened. Take the case of Barbara.

Barbara was a terrible sport. She cheated at everything in order to win. When she lost, she felt really awful, as if the world were going to end.

You've heard about terrible sports who hit other people or insult them over games. Barbara did that every now and then. But more often she just went off and sulked if she lost a game. She felt shaky and sick. The whole world seemed to be laughing at her. Barbara just had to win at everything.

One day Barbara lost a card game with her sister Elaine. She threw the cards all over the floor. "This is a stupid game!" she yelled. "I never win! Never!"

"Come on, don't throw a fit about it," said Elaine. "Good grief, don't cry! What's the matter?"

Barbara started to cry angry tears that just made her feel worse. "I never win a thing!" she sobbed. "You and Mom, you're always against me! You do everything better than me and make fun of me!"

"Where did you get an idea like that?" asked Elaine. "You're the go-getter in this family. You're the one who gets good grades and practices so hard to win games."

"Yeah, but that's because *you* don't have to work hard. Everything is easy for you."

As Barbara said that, she realized that it wasn't true at all. Things weren't easy for Elaine. She had to struggle through her homework for hours every night. And she had just had a fight with her boyfriend. But inside Barbara's head, a voice was saying, "She can do anything! Everything's easy for her!"

"Oh, forget it," said Barbara, and she went to her room. "Why do I think everything's easy for her?" she kept wondering. "And why do I get so mad?"

Barbara couldn't answer her own question. But after that, she began to watch Elaine and her mother. She had always thought they could do everything perfectly. Now she saw there were a lot of things they couldn't do perfectly. There were also many things she could do better than they could!

Barbara realized that, all her life, she'd thought Elaine and her mother were so smart and strong that she could never catch up to them. She felt as if she'd been born weak and stupid because she couldn't do things as well as they could. She felt *different from* the way she thought she should be.

That was why Barbara had to win at everything. She was trying to prove that she really was as "good" as she thought she ought to be—as good as Elaine and her mother were.

Sometimes Barbara's problem happens in a different way. Sometimes you feel different from what your parents *want* you to be. That was the trouble Joe and his brothers had.

Joe was the oldest of four boys. If you didn't know them very well, you'd think they had one problem: they hated all small living creatures.

They hated dogs. They hated cats. They hated other kids. (Naturally they didn't have any friends.) They even hated each other. If you had gone to their house, you would have heard yelling and name-calling and crying from morning until night.

A closer look at Joe and his brothers would have revealed what was really wrong with them: they were afraid. But Joe and his brothers tried to hide their fear by pretending to be mean and angry.

What were Joe and his brothers really afraid of?

Dogs, cats and children. But why? Well, dogs, cats and children have one thing in common—they all have to be taken care of. And taking care of pets and children isn't easy. They're noisy and messy. If you've ever heard a cat crying for food or a baby screaming for attention, you know how irritating they can be.

Joe's parents knew it too. One child is hard enough to take care of, but four is a tremendous job! As you can imagine, Joe's parents complained about it.

"Don't you kids ever shut up?" they'd ask. If the kids were impatient for dinner, their mother yelled, "What do you think I am, your slave?" And if Joe and his brothers complained about having to do work around the house, their parents naturally got mad. "After all we do for you," they'd say, "you won't do one little thing for us!"

Joe and his brothers pretended not to care what their parents said about them. Once, when their mother asked if they thought she was their slave, Joe yelled, "Yeah! Cook, slave!" Secretly, though, the boys were terrified of their parents' complaints.

You can imagine what Joe thought to himself about their complaining. "My parents don't really like me," he told himself. "Look at all the work they do for me. There must be something wrong with somebody who's so much trouble. My parents couldn't have *wanted* me to be this way. I'm a mistake—no good."

Joe, like Barbara, was afraid he was "different." He thought he shouldn't be noisy and messy. His image of what he should be was very different from the real Joe. The image was clean and quiet and always did what his parents told him to. In fact, Joe's image was more like a doll than a real child.

Joe knew he couldn't act like the image. He would always be *some* trouble for his parents until he grew up. He couldn't help it. So he grew frightened. What if his parents got tired of all the work they had to do for him? What if they stopped taking care of him? Joe just couldn't keep from worrying about it.

That was why Joe couldn't stand pets and children. They reminded him of himself. And they reminded him of his fear that he was too much trouble for his parents. So, whenever Joe saw a pet or a child, he was afraid.

What Joe didn't realize was that all kids are a lot of trouble—and that parents are human and are apt to complain. But this doesn't mean parents really believe kids should always behave perfectly. That would make children easier to take care of, but it wouldn't be very interesting.

If Joe had understood that his parents didn't really want him to be perfect, his feelings about himself would have changed. He would have seen there was nothing so terrible about the way he was.

Most fears of "being different" starts like Joe's and Barbara's. They start when you want to be something you can't be. Or when you're different from the way your parents seem to want you to be. There are many things your parents can seem to expect of you. If you can't be those things, you feel "different."

To list the things people think they should be would take a lot of space. Some people think they should be very smart. Some think they should be friends with everyone. Some think they should be tough. One of the most frustrating ideas is one girls sometimes have. They think they are "wrong" because they aren't boys.

Like most fears, this fear of being "different" because you're a girl is usually hidden, especially from you. Everyone's heard of "tomboys." But most girls who feel "different" because they are girls don't act tomboyish. They just feel and act like other frightened people. For instance, let's look at the case of Ellen.

Ellen had a brother named Ralph. He made her furious. He was only a year older than she was, but he had a lot more freedom than she did. And he got more encouragement from his parents.

When Ralph got good grades, his parents were really happy. They hugged him and got all excited. Ellen's parents praised her for getting good grades, but they didn't seem very thrilled about it.

In the same way, Ellen's parents were happy if Ralph won a fight at school. But when Ellen hit a girl who had called her names, they made her stay in all day Saturday.

Ralph didn't have to make his bed or clean up his room. Ellen did. She had to iron some of her clothes and wash the dishes, too.

Worst of all, Ralph could just take off with his friends on Saturdays. Ellen's mother always asked *her* a lot of questions about where she was going and what time she'd be back.

Ellen sometimes felt miserable about this unfair treatment. But she thought she deserved it because she was "wrong." She wasn't a boy. So she never asked her parents to change it. She just went on being unhappy a lot of the time. And she avoided thinking about why she was unhappy.

Sometimes, when Ellen was saddest, she daydreamed about being very brave. In one daydream, she was on an expedition to the jungle and had saved the whole safari from monsters. People heard about her bravery and put her picture in the newspapers and on TV. But this daydream just made her sadder when it was over. "Me, save anybody?" she thought "I'd probably just pass out."

Then, one Christmas, Ellen and Ralph visited their aunt and uncle, Trudy and Jim. (Ellen's mother was sick and she decided it would be a dreary Christmas for the children if they stayed home.)

Aunt Trudy and Uncle Jim had a big family—three boys and a girl. Christmas at her house was noisy and happy, like a party that lasted three or four days. And almost as soon as she'd arrived, Ellen got her first surprise.

"Hey, Ralph!" called Ellen's cousin Mark, who was thirteen. "You wanta help me chop up some greens?"

"Greens?" asked Ralph. "*Cooking?*" His eyes were wide. "That's girls' work!"

"You're not afraid, are you?" Mark teased him. "Or maybe it's too hard?"

"You better do what he says," joked Mark's brother, Don. "He gets mean when he's got a knife."

"Okay, okay." Ralph put on an apron, and tried to cut greens. At first he looked like a prince who'd been told to take care of the pigs. But when he saw how fast Mark worked and how well he did the job, his face changed.

Ellen almost laughed out loud. She knew it would be a wonderful holiday.

And it was—even for Ralph. He got to like the way

the boys kidded each other around in the kitchen. Uncle Jim liked to cook his own special recipes for big dinners. And his sons helped him in the kitchen because he seemed to be having so much fun.

Ellen spent most of the days talking to her cousin Katie, who was her age. When the girls wanted to go to the movies together, Aunt Trudy just said, "Sure." And Ellen found out that Katie had been in fights at school and never gotten in trouble.

"Why should I get in trouble?" asked Katie. "If somebody hits you, you've got to defend yourself."

On the last day of the visit, Ellen found herself talking to Aunt Trudy. She told her she'd enjoyed her visit and that she thought Ralph had too.

Aunt Trudy laughed. "Poor Ralph. I thought he'd turn green when my boys made him help in the kitchen. He is just like your Dad. He wouldn't be caught dead doing 'women's work.'"

"I never knew men did things around the house," said Ellen.

"Well, neither did I, until I married Jim," said Aunt Trudy. "Jim's great. He and I share nearly everything. The fun as well as the work."

"My father doesn't feel like that," said Ellen.

"No," said Aunt Trudy, "I'm afraid your father had a hard time. There were five of us girls in the family. He was the only boy. So he's always drawn very careful lines between what girls are supposed to be like and what boys are supposed to be like."

"Aunt Trudy," said Ellen carefully, a little scared, "do you think maybe my parents are unfair with me? I mean, I feel like Ralph gets to do everything and I can't do anything."

72

"Oh, I'm sure they are," said Aunt Trudy cheerfully. "Your father's a strict person, especially with girls. You'll live through it. But I'll tell you one thing: don't let it get you down. You can take care of yourself as well as Ralph can, any time."

"Do you think that's true?" said Ellen.

"Sure. Look at Katie. She can handle things as well as any of her brothers could at her age."

Ellen thought about what Aunt Trudy had said. She just couldn't believe it. Did Aunt Trudy really think she could take care of herself as well as Ralph could?

Of course I can, thought Ellen. I *know* I can. But she still didn't quite believe it. And that was the problem.

Ellen felt just the way Barbara and Joe did—not good enough. Her image of what she should be involved being something she *couldn't* be—a boy.

Because Ellen thought she should be a boy, and wasn't, she felt as if she was the wrong kind of person. She was afraid no one would ever like her—they'd wish she was a boy. And because she thought boys were "better" she imagined they could do *everything* better than she could. Even though she hated the way Ralph was allowed more freedom than she was, she secretly believed he deserved it.

When Ellen saw that Aunt Trudy and Uncle Jim seemed to think she was as "good" as Ralph, Ellen began to feel better about herself. Maybe being a girl wasn't the wrong thing after all.

Ellen visited Aunt Trudy and Uncle Jim at the next vacation and that summer too. She and Katie became good friends. Ellen also tried to persuade her parents to let her do as much as Ralph did. She didn't have much luck there. Ellen felt bad about being refused, but she wasn't desperate, the way she'd been before. She felt that at least some people liked her the way she was.

If you feel that no one likes you the way you are—that you're "the wrong kind of person"—you'll be unhappy as Barbara, Joe and Ellen were. You may also take those unhappy feelings out on other people. This is called prejudice.

Prejudice is a very common feeling. Actually it's just another example of projection. Let's say I feel "out of it." I think I'm different, wrong, bad. You come along and you're different from me. You don't dress the same way I do. You don't think the same way I do. So I project my feelings about myself on to you. I say to myself, "I'm not different. He's the one who's weird. Look at his clothes. Look at the way he acts. What a jerk!" Of course, that's really the way I feel about myself. But instead of admitting it, I take it out on you.

Naturally everyone is a little afraid, at first, of people who are very different from himself. These people seem unfamiliar. But once you get to know them, you can see they are human beings with feelings—including friendly feelings.

Prejudiced people can't realize this. They are afraid to get to know anyone who is different from themselves. All they can think about is the difference. That is because *they* feel "different."

Remember this if you decide to make fun of someone because he is different from you. Do *you* feel different, too?

And if someone makes fun of you for wearing strange clothes or acting odd, remember that *he* is probably the one who feels odd. He's just trying to make himself feel better by making you feel worse.

Once you realize that the fear of being different starts with you—that the difference is between you and an image of yourself in your head—you can conquer your fear. Try to find out why you feel "different." Do you think you should be more like your parents? Your sisters or brothers? Should you be older? Should you be tougher, or more gentle? And once you know what you think you should be, ask yourself if there's any *good reason* you should be that way. Will it make you a better person? Will it really make you happier? Can you be that way, even if you really want to?

Once you're able to recognize that the image in your head isn't the way you *have* to be, you'll see that you're not so "different" after all. A lot of people would like to be things they're not. And once you've decided what you'd really like to be, you may find you're a lot closer to it than you guessed.

So get to know yourself. You may make a valuable and helpful friend.

CHAPTER EIGHT
WHAT YOU CAN DO

There's a lot more to most fears than you realize. And many fears start for reasons that you'd never think of at first. You've seen it in the stories in earlier chapters.

Remember Caroline? It took her a long time to realize that she wasn't afraid of dirt, but of her own anger. And Grace would never have guessed that she wasn't afraid of the dark, but of the way it made her feel—lonely and abandoned. That's why most fears are so hard to fight.

You've probably thought you've lost something, for instance, your wristwatch—and, after taking your whole room apart, found it on your wrist. That's what a lot of fears are like. You look everywhere for the thing that scares you, but you miss the closest place—inside yourself.

When you're afraid, try looking inside yourself first. You're much more likely to be afraid of your own feelings than of any danger outside yourself. There just aren't that many dangers around.

Remember, too, that you may not quite know you're afraid. You may just worry a lot. You may bite your nails or fidget without realizing it. You get so used to feeling tense that you forget what it's like to be relaxed and happy.

There's a lot you can do to fight the fear of your own feelings. We've said it before but it won't hurt to say it again. FIND OUT WHAT YOU'RE REALLY AFRAID OF. If you're anxious about something harmless, like dirt, stop and think.

Think about the object, person, or event that scares you. Has it always scared you? What's so frightening about it? What does it remind you of? Chances are that it will remind you of some strong feeling of your own—one you don't like.

Another way to learn about your fears is to watch your family. Suppose you're afraid of dogs. Do your parents like dogs? Or are they afraid of dogs themselves? It's likely that dogs mean something important to your parents. That's why they're important to you.

If you can't figure out what you're really afraid of by yourself, try talking to someone you trust. After all, thinking about your fears isn't easy. You tend to feel the bad things you imagine might really happen if you think about them. So you'll feel safer if someone else is with you when you bring your fears to light.

Once you discover the feelings that really frighten you, you can take action. Frightening feelings are likely to be one of these:

Loneliness and Helplessness. We saw these feelings in the case of Grace, who was afraid of the dark. We also saw them in the case of Terry, who was afraid his parents would leave him to go away with strangers. Harold and Priscilla, in chapters four and five, were also afraid they were helpless and alone. And Lucy, in chapter six, was afraid to learn arithmetic because she thought her sister would leave her if she did.

If you feel abandoned—all alone—you may be afraid ever to be by yourself. Being in the dark, being in a big crowd of strangers, being left on your own—all those things will scare you.

Try to understand why you feel abandoned. Do you feel your parents don't care about you? Why shouldn't they care? Is it because you feel you're not as good as they want you to be? Do they seem to be more interested in their work or in their friends than in you?

Try talking to your parents about all this. You can probably learn about their feelings—and they can learn from yours. You may find out you're not as alone as you think.

Anger. You remember Roger's anger in chapter three. He was mad at his parents for spending all their time with strangers. Frank and Denise, in chapter four, and Jack and Jeff, in chapter five, were angry too. And they were all afraid of their anger.

If you are angry—really angry, like the children in these stories—you may be afraid to be with other people. You may be afraid people are watching you. You may forget what people ask you to do, or you may always seem to be bumping into people or stepping on them.

Try to find out just what makes you angry. Do you feel your parents are leaving you out? Are your brothers and sisters getting more attention than you are? Do they make you angry by picking on you or teasing you?

You're probably afraid of getting angry because you're afraid you'll hurt someone. Then you'll be in real trouble. But, after all, you can *tell* someone you're mad, and why you're mad, without hitting him or breaking his things. Then you'll feel better and he might stop making you mad.

If he won't listen, there's a lot you can do to "take out" your anger. Do some really hard work—the kind where you can hit things or dig. Throw some rocks at a tin can.

Or, if you're not the violent type, you can try something different. You can make up daydreams to let out the anger you feel. Daydreams about monsters, witches, storms and disasters, or just plain mean people are useful. When you imagine yourself growling and spitting fire, you use up the energy that goes into being angry and then you feel better.

If you've ever read any fairy tales, you'll see that people have been making up stories about anger for a long time. Think of all the witches, dragons, and trolls in those stories. Think of television cartoons, where characters always push one another off cliffs or hit each other in the head. People are dealing with their anger by making up those cartoons.

Wanting Something. We saw the problems of wanting something you think you shouldn't have in Sandy's story. Sandy wanted to take her mother's place at home. And George, in chapter three, wanted friends but was afraid to have them.

Once you've realized what you want, you have to try to stop feeling guilty about it. Chances are that the thing you want isn't so terrible. What would be wrong, for instance, with George having friends? What's wrong with Sandy wanting a family of her own? Try to understand why you feel guilty about what you want.

Sometimes you really can't have what you want right away. Sandy, for instance, couldn't kick her mother out and take over her family. In that case, try to think of a good substitute for the thing you want. It you were Sandy, you could do baby-sitting or volunteer work taking care of children.

So—the feeling you're afraid of is probably like one of the feelings in this list. If you can find out which it is and let it out, you can overcome your fear.

But what if you've tried and tried to help yourself and failed? Then there's one more way to help yourself. You can visit a psychiatrist.

A psychiatrist is a doctor who knows about the way the mind works. (He may also be called a counselor, a therapist, a clinical psychologist, or a psychoanalyst.) He helps you get over fears as a regular doctor might help you get over a cough.

When you see a psychiatrist, you usually talk to him for about an hour a week, sometimes more often, sometimes less. He asks you to talk about your feelings. You can talk to him about problems in your home, in school, or with your friends. You start by talking about the things you seem to fear. Then together, you and the psychiatrist try to discover what feelings these things call to mind.

Many people think psychiatrists only help people who are "crazy." Some people are afraid to go to a psychiatrist. But, actually, psychiatric treatment can help almost everyone. It is, after all, just another way to learn about yourself. Most people who visit psychiatrists are not crazy.

Sometimes, learning about yourself is hard. It's hard to realize you have all these angry, scary feelings. But the more you learn about these feelings, the better you can fight them. And if you gain confidence by fighting them, you'll have more good feelings to balance the ones that scare you.

GLOSSARY

GLOSSARY

Abandonment: Being left completely alone without anyone to help you when you need it.

Anger: The emotion we feel when we think we have been hurt, treated unfairly, or stopped from doing what we want to do.

Anxiety: A feeling of fear when we are not actually in danger.

Association: A connection. We make an association when one idea, thing or person reminds us of another idea, thing, or person.

Attention: The care and concern we get from and give to other people.

Authority: The power to give orders and make other people obey them.

Bravery: The ability to overcome fear.

Caution: The act of being careful until you find out whether or not you are in danger.

Confidence: Belief in your ability to do the things you want to, and have to, do.

Counselor: A person who understands the emotional side of school problems and can help to solve them.

Curiosity: A natural desire to learn what things are and how they work.

Daydreams:	Stories you imagine that contain feelings and wishes about yourself and others.
Dread:	Looking forward to something with great fear.
Dreams:	The thoughts and feelings that go through a sleeping person's mind.
Emotion:	Any specific feeling. Love, hate, anger, joy are emotions.
Failure:	Not being able to do something we want to, or have to, do.
Fear:	The emotion we feel when we are in danger.
Feeling:	An emotion; a mental response we have to a person, thing or idea.
Guilt:	The feeling of having done something wrong.
Image:	The mental picture we have of what we're supposed to be like.
Loneliness:	The feeling that no one cares about or wants to be with us.
Nervous:	Restless, not calm.
Nightmare:	A dream that frightens us.
Prejudice:	Disliking someone or something because it's different from the people and things you're used to.

Projection:	Imagining that our own feelings are actually coming from someone else.
Psychiatrist:	A doctor who helps people who are unhappy because of feelings they have hidden, even from themselves.
Punishment:	The pain or loss we suffer when we have done something wrong.
School Phobia:	Fear of school, the building, the teachers, the other children, or being away from home.
Shame:	The act of feeling bad about ourselves because we think we have done something wrong.
Stranger:	Any person we don't know.
Success:	Being able to do the things we have to, or want to, do.
Tense:	Prepared to face danger.
Worry:	To feel troubled or uneasy.

INDEX

INDEX

abandonment, 11–12, 14–15,
   43, 45, 78
   definition of, 85
   see also divorce
anger, 4
   combating, 78–79
   definition of, 85
   projecting, 19, 21, 27, 36
   suppressing, 7, 11–12, 18, 21,
      33–36, 50
   toward parents, 6–7, 11–12,
      19–21
animals
   cats, 67–69
   dogs, 2–3, 67–69, 77
   humans changed into, 56
   imaginary, 11
anxiety
   definition of 3–4, 85
   overcoming, 4–8
   see also specific anxieties
association, definition of 85
attention
   definition of, 85
   lack of, from parents, 16–
      17, 19–20, 44–45, 78
authority, 30–40
   definition of, 85
   see also parents, policemen,
      teachers

babies: *see* sexual curiosity,
   siblings
being different: *see* different,
   fear of being

boys
   girls' desire to be, 70–74
   see also siblings
bravery, definition of, 85
brothers: *see* siblings

cats, 67–69
caution, definition of, 85
changes, 56
choking, 50–51
cleanliness, 4–8
clinical psychologists: *see* psychiatrists
confidence, definition of, 85
counselors
   definition of, 85
   see also psychiatrists
criticism, 35
curiosity, definition of, 85
   see also sexual curiosity

darkness, 9–13
daydreams
   as way to combat anger, 79
   definition of, 86
desertion: *see* abandonment
different, fear of being, 63–75
dirt, 4–8
disease: *see* sickness
divorce, 37–38
   see also abandonment
doctors, 27
   see also psychiatrists
dogs, 2–3, 67–69, 77
dread, definition of, 86

91